MARTHA WATSON ALLPRESS

Martha Watson Allpress is a writer and actor from Lincolnshire
in the East Midlands, now based in South East London. Her
upbringing, in a place defined by its lack of definition, trickles
into her love of murky, complicated characters and stories.

Patricia Gets Ready was her debut play and ran at the White
Bear Theatre in Kennington in 2019, before transferring the next
year to the VAULT Festival, from there to the 2021 Edinburgh
Fringe and onto a 2022 tour. It is now being developed for
screen.

Her second full length play, *Kick*, was winner of the 2022 Bill
Cashmore Award, and was presented at the Lyric Hammersmith
for a limited run. Her shorter works include *Wild Swim*
(Papatango), *Call Me Maybe* (Arcola) and *Contains Adult
Themes and Violence* (Gatehouse).

Martha is part of Hampstead Theatre's INSPIRE Playwrighting
Group and is working toward a new show with their
dramaturgical support. She was also one of the 2021/22 cohort
of BIFA's Springboard programme.

Through her writing, Martha aims to explore the nuances of
humanity, crack some jokes, and play as many banging tunes as
possible.

Other Titles in This Series

Annie Baker
THE ANTIPODES
THE FLICK
JOHN

Lily Bevan
ZOO & TWELVE COMIC MONOLOGUES
  FOR WOMEN

Jessie Cave
SUNRISE

Karen Cogan
DRIP FEED & THE HALF OF IT

Caitríona Daly
DUCK DUCK GOOSE

Phoebe Eclair-Powell
DORAIN *with* Owen Horsley
EPIC LOVE AND POP SONGS
FURY
HARM
WINK

Sophie Ellerby
LIT

Natasha Gordon
NINE NIGHT

Rose Heiney
ELEPHANTS
ORIGINAL DEATH RABBIT

Tatty Hennessy
A HUNDRED WORDS FOR SNOW
SOMETHING AWFUL

Nicôle Lecky
SUPERHOE

Laura Lomas
BIRD & OTHER MONOLOGUES FOR
  YOUNG WOMEN
CHAOS

Benedict Lombe
LAVA

Cordelia Lynn
HEDDA TESMAN *after* Ibsen
LELA & CO.
LOVE AND OTHER ACTS OF VIOLENCE
ONE FOR SORROW
THREE SISTERS *after* Chekhov

Lucy Kirkwood
BEAUTY AND THE BEAST *with* Katie Mitchell
BLOODY WIMMIN
THE CHILDREN
CHIMERICA
HEDDA *after* Ibsen
IT FELT EMPTY WHEN THE HEART WENT
  AT FIRST BUT IT IS ALRIGHT NOW
LUCY KIRKWOOD PLAYS: ONE
MOSQUITOES
NSFW
TINDERBOX
THE WELKIN

Suzie Miller
PRIMA FACIE

Henry Naylor
ARABIAN NIGHTMARES

Margaret Perry
COLLAPSIBLE

Winsome Pinnock
LEAVE TAKING
ROCKETS AND BLUE LIGHTS
TAKEN
TITUBA

Lauryn Redding
BLOODY ELLE

Stuart Slade
BU21
CANS
GLEE & ME

Stef Smith
ENOUGH
GIRL IN THE MACHINE
HUMAN ANIMALS
NORA : A DOLL'S HOUSE
REMOTE
SWALLOW

Ciara Elizabeth Smyth
SAUCE & ALL HONEY

Izzy Tennyson
GROTTY & BRUTE

debbie tucker green
BORN BAD
DEBBIE TUCKER GREEN PLAYS: ONE
DIRTY BUTTERFLY
EAR FOR EYE
HANG
NUT
A PROFOUNDLY AFFECTIONATE,
  PASSIONATE DEVOTION TO SOMEONE
  (–NOUN)
RANDOM
STONING MARY
TRADE & GENERATIONS
TRUTH AND RECONCILIATION

Various
15 HEROINES: 15 MONOLOGUES ADAPTED
  FROM OVID
HERETIC VOICES
THE MOTHERHOOD PROJECT
SNATCHES: MOMENTS FROM 100 YEARS
  OF WOMEN'S LIVES

Phoebe Waller-Bridge
FLEABAG

Camilla Whitehill
MR INCREDIBLE

Sophie Wu
RAMONA TELLS JIM

Martha Watson Allpress

PATRICIA GETS READY
(FOR A DATE WITH THE MAN THAT USED TO HIT HER)

NICK HERN BOOKS
London
www.nickhernbooks.co.uk

A Nick Hern Book

Patricia Gets Ready (for a date with the man that used to hit her) first published in Great Britain as a paperback original in 2022 by Nick Hern Books Limited, The Glasshouse, 49a Goldhawk Road, London W12 8QP

Patricia Gets Ready (for a date with the man that used to hit her) copyright © 2022 Martha Watson Allpress

Martha Watson Allpress has asserted her right to be identified as the author of this work

Cover image: Heedayah Lockman

Designed and typeset by Nick Hern Books, London
Printed in Great Britain by Mimeo Ltd, Huntingdon, Cambridgeshire PE29 6XX

A CIP catalogue record for this book is available from the British Library

ISBN 978 1 83904 090 0

Woodland CARBON
www.woodlandcarbon.co.uk
NICK HERN BOOKS
Printed on Carbon Captured paper

A quick note from Martha, writer

When I left my ex-boyfriend, I did not say his name out loud for at least five years. This is the only way I can articulate the sheer mess of trauma recovery. I could not say a man's name out loud.

Around nine-ish years ago I was with a very nasty man, in a very complicated relationship. Around eight-ish years ago I left this very nasty man, and embarked on a new, complicated relationship with myself. With my 'new self', and trying desperately to make peace that I'd let my 'old self' die. Still so young, and still so hurt, I turned to art. I have a habit of doing that when life gets messy. I believe in the social responsibility of art. That us – those awful beings that call ourselves artists – have a duty to reflect and decipher life in all its unpleasant and chaotic glory. I searched for myself in the stories of others, and then I got pissed off.

Trauma survivors in art, especially those such as myself who had emerged from abusive relationships, were frail, apologetic and diminutive. They were all middle-aged, skinny and quiet. They were so quiet. They were voiceless. But eight-ish years ago, there I was, still funny, still enjoying sex, still moving through the world as a very fleshed-out person. To be skinny, middle-aged and quiet are valid things, they are allowed, of course, but they are categorically not the only options. I searched for post-trauma self-care. I was presented with face masks and bubble baths. Art failed me, and that is something I could not allow.

Patricia Gets Ready (for a date with the man that used to hit her) is a stream of consciousness. It is an uneven mood swing. It is an unsafe lullaby. It is what I wish was available to me all those years ago. I wish deeply that eight-ish years ago there was a play, screaming at me that EMPOWERMENT IS NOT THE DESTINATION, IT IS THE JOURNEY TO SOMETHING NEW. I wish eight-ish years ago I'd been embraced by a character like Patricia, showing me that surviving an abusive relationship is not a personality trait. I wish eight-ish years ago I'd learned that trauma recovery informs you, it does not become you. Because maybe, *maybe*, then, it would not have taken me over eight years to stop being terrified of his name. Eight years to throw that name around like the nothing it is.

I am eternally grateful to Kaleya, Khai, and all the others involved in the evolution of the show, and for the delicacy and gentleness you have offered it. The kindness of this team has set the bar so high for all future creative endeavours, and has emboldened me to act with radical empathy and care.

I loved him a lot.

And now I truly, truly hope… that he's dead under a truck.

Garbage prick.

With huge thanks to:

Tender UK for the phenomenal support with the script and production, for each and every iteration of our show.

The White Bear Theatre, VAULT Festival, The Pleasance, Brixton House and our 2022 tour venues for believing this play deserves an audience.

The *Patricia* team throughout the years: Angelina Chudi, Kaleya Baxe, Nur Khairiyah, Yasmin Dawes, Abs Sol, Beth Duke, Ella Clarke, Jessica Brigham, Leon Smith, Layla Madanat, Xanthus, Korey J Ryan, Heedayah Lockman, Greta Mitchell, Steven Frost, Ben Ralph, Libby Mai and Remi King; for truly everything. Everything. It's beyond words and gratitude.

Amy Sparks at United Agents for the support, belief and voice notes.

Christopher Michael Hough for the good love.

&

Young Vic Taking Part, NDT Broadgate, Alford House, Nic Connaughton and Chloé Nelkin, Open Door, HighTide, Hackney Showroom.

To Cathy Hobbs, Johnny Hobbs, Christopher Watson and Sue Bell for only ever being encouraging. Encouraging an active love of reading, encouraging a lack of embarrassment at having ambition, and encouraging me to know I am worthy of rest (a swim and a Pringle sandwich always).

To Pamela Allpress for being the coolest person that's ever existed.

A quick note from Kaleya, director

In many ways, *Patricia Gets Ready* is the play I have always dreamt of.

From the age of fourteen, by some miracle, I ended up joining the youth board of Tender Education and Arts, even if mainly for the free snacks. The charity's mission: to teach young people about healthy relationships and domestic abuse through the art of drama. To empower people to prevent or at least minimise the violence in relationships before it's too late, if possible. The knowledge I learnt was invaluable; not just in terms of spotting early warning signs but also how to help yourself and others who can so easily and accidentally give their love to the wrong person. I carry these lessons with me every day and I would advise anyone to explore their work or this topic more.

Tender was the first place I discovered the power of drama. To understand that there are many ways to learn outside of reading a textbook. To feel empowered when playing out a scenario safely. To realise how deeply we can be affected by art that is emotive. To experience the healing, joy and community that participatory arts can create.

I went on to study Applied Theatre to become a facilitator that could use drama as an educational and social tool. I continued working with Tender, and as a writer too. I dreamed of one day writing a play that would enlighten and destroy all the characteristics and stereotypes around abusive relationships. Who knew that the entire time I was manifesting *Patricia Gets Ready* as the first full-length play I would direct – it couldn't have been any other way.

Not only am I proud of how many hearts this little show has touched, but how our small team has approached every element with compassion and kindness. Personally, it has also been important to cast Patricia as a Black Woman and bring my community to the forefront of an issue they are overproportionately affected by, yet underrepresented in.

Theatre can save lives – and many times has. I am forever grateful to Tender for touching my life and many others; Martha for writing a character who is complicated, layered and very human; and to Khai and the team who understood the heart of this story before there was any money or hype to evidence it. *Patricia Gets Ready* really is the play I have always dreamed of. I hope, as you meet Martha's honest, textured and poetic words, you see why.

A quick note from Khai, producer

Patricia Gets Ready will always hold a special place in my life as it was the first play that I produced in London. Right from the beginning, I knew this play was special (and I could not believe that it was Martha's debut play!). It's an urgent piece that does not stereotype survivors of domestic abuse. Patricia is not a victim; she is confident, sexy and fearless. She is a strong woman. And whether we've been in abusive relationships or not, we all can relate to her.

This play has had a remarkable journey. From the first show at the White Bear Theatre, to me coming on board as producer for the VAULT Festival in 2020, to being awarded the Charlie Hartill Development Fund for Artists of Colour to present the show at the 2020 Edinburgh Fringe – which got cancelled because of the Covid pandemic, before eventually presenting it at the 2021 edition – to going on a UK tour in 2022; *Patricia Gets Ready* has and will continue to amaze and impact audiences. But it's not only the audience that have been impacted by the play. In the course of producing this play, I have learned a tremendous amount about safeguarding and collective caring, in how to hold the team working on the production and the audience as a producer. So thank you *Patricia Gets Ready* for making me a better producer.

I'm very excited for this next development of *Patricia Gets Ready*. It has been an exciting journey and I know that it will continue to amaze and impact audiences positively. Congratulations to Martha and every single person who has had a hand in getting the play to where it is today.

Tender

Tender is an arts charity working with young people to prevent domestic abuse, and sexual violence, through creative projects.

0207 697 4277
tender.org.uk

Bright Sky App

Bright Sky is a mobile app and website for anyone experiencing domestic abuse, or who is worried about someone else. The app can be downloaded free from the app stores.

bright-sky.org.uk

Refuge

Refuge run a 24-hour, free-to-call helpline for anyone experiencing, or concerned, about domestic abuse.

0808 2000 247
refuge.org.uk

Patricia Gets Ready (for a date with the man that used to hit her) was first performed at VAULT Festival, London, in February 2020, before a run at the Edinburgh Festival Fringe in August 2021. The creative team was as follows:

PATRICIA	Angelina Chudi
Writer	Martha Watson Allpress
Director	Kaleya Baxe
Producer	Nur Khairiyah (Khai)
Sound Designer	Beth Duke
Set and Costume Designer	Ella Clarke
Lighting	Steven Frost

Patricia Gets Ready (for a date with the man that used to hit her) was revived at Mercury Theatre Colchester on 10 May 2022, before touring the UK, including a run at Brixton House, London. The creative team was as follows:

PATRICIA   Yasmin Dawes

Writer   Martha Watson Allpress
Director   Kaleya Baxe
Producer   Nur Khairiyah (Khai)
Production Stage Manager   Leon Smith
Well-being Practitioner   Abs Sol
Assistant Producer   Layla Madanat
Set and Costume Designer   Ella Clarke
Sound Designer   Beth Duke
Lighting Designer   Jessica Brigham

Character

PATRICIA, *early twenties*

Lives with her mum in her hometown. Cycle courier. Not a person fuelled by career or financial ambitions, but a person who roots for love and joy. Patricia was in a physically abusive relationship for two years and has been out of it for one year. She refuses to let this be something that defines her, but it has inevitably hardened her.

Notes

The play takes place inside Patricia's bedroom; however, all that needs to be signified to the audience is the space she's in is safe to her.

Any time the play is presented, it should be done so with kindness and care at the centre of that process. This includes ensuring all audience have access to helplines and trigger warnings.

This text went to press before the end of rehearsals and so may differ slightly from the play as performed.

15

1 p.m.

Outside.

PATRICIA *stands alone. Shocked.*

> Shit.
>
> Hi.
>
> Oh my God.
>
> Hi, no I've said that.
>
> Hi.

Pause.

> I... I um... I didn't know you were back. I just –
>
> no you go –
>
> I just wasn't expecting to see you.
>
> When did you get back? You didn't tell me?
>
> That's great. I just wasn't expecting to see you.
>
> Permanently? Sorry, didn't mean to cut you off but, permanently?
>
> Oh.
>
> No, that's great.
>
> Yeah.
>
> Yeah, good for you, that's great.
>
> I'm good. I'm really good. Really good.
>
> Same old, same old really.

Yep, still cycling.

Good for the head. Clear head, you know?

No, actually no, I've... um. I'm still with Mum.

Beat.

Still need looking after.

Pause.

She looks at her shaking hands.

I had... I had so much I wanted to say to you. It's literally all gone. I just... I just didn't know. I wish I'd known.

Pause.

I'm not making a scene?

I'm not angry. Well I am. I am very angry. But I'm not getting angry. Okay?

I'm not making a fucking scene.

Christ! Can you – I swear to God –

Pause.

Sorry.

Beat.

Look, can I –

– no, I need to interrupt –

Well I think I can so...

Enough!

I don't...

I'm going to go now.

Yeah.

I need to um… bye.

PATRICIA *goes to exit…*

What?

I mean no, I don't, but…

I just don't think that's a good idea.

I don't…

Okay.

Okay, half eight. Okay.

I'll see you there.

Goodbye.

Pause.

Shit. Shit. Shit. Shit. Shit. Shit. Shit. Shit. Shit.

PATRICIA *has a panic attack.*

4 p.m.

Inside.

Shit. Shit. Shit. Shit. Shit. Shit. Shit. Shit. Shit.

ARGHHHHHHHHHHHHHHHHHHHHHHH.

Jesus it wasn't like I was unprepared. Not like I haven't imagined that conversation over and over and over. FUCK ME. I have had a speech planned for a goddamn year. And it's beautiful. It is so good; the aggression, the burns, just the general

tone. It's so suave and sophisticated, like proper...
'I am a woman and I define me...' I have been
crafting that shit in daydreams and showers and
cycling... and I said 'hi.' THREE TIMES. I really
feel like one would have been enough, if not too
many. But, wow, well done me, three times. That's
just... that's so... yeah.

Patricia 'hi hi hi' Eleanor Williams.

That's just great. Great. No, no, no, that's exactly
how I wanted it to go. Really the assertive image I
wanted to leave him with. Yeah, I'm really fucking
sure he sees how much of a grown-ass woman I am
now. Doesn't think of me as little now. Definitely
not weak any more! Christ!

And dinner? Oh yes mate I'd love to go to dinner
with you, can think of nothing I'd rather do. Three
courses, let's get a tasting menu, looking forward
to it. I MEAN COME ON.

Why do – why do – why do you betray yourself
like that? I mean, I knew, my brain knew, what I
wanted to say but it just... couldn't.

Coward.

I feel so angry. I feel SO angry.

Fucking coward.

This is so deeply embarrassing. I can't believe I
couldn't... After all this time, it's been enough
time, I can't believe I just couldn't...

I could just not show up. Stand him up. Of course
that is the clever, high-ground, middle-finger
option, but... well we all know I'm going to go. If
I can't even say 'fuck you' to the man, then I'm not
going to leave him sat alone at a restaurant am I.

No. I said hello to him three times, I'm not going to stand him up.

I could say it to him at the restaurant. I could say it all to him at the restaurant.

Would that be making a scene?

I feel like if I spoke really low and calmly it'd be like, even more powerful, even more... umph. You know? Yeah. Yeah. That'd be really good, and get it all out before he even orders so I can just storm out and leave him lonely and embarrassed and hungry.

Unless he's already ordered before I arrive? At least drinks. There'll be drinks on the table. God! That is such a him move. He's such a... such a...

They'll be two fucking Negronis on the table, I'd put money on it.

Coward. Jesus.

Coward. Noun. A person who is contemptibly lacking in the courage to do or endure dangerous or unpleasant things.

ARGHHHHHHHHHHHHHHHHHHHHHHHHH.

Shit.

PATRICIA *gets in the shower and wraps a towel round her head.*

She listens to 'Self' by Noname.

PATRICIA *applies face creams/body creams, etc... until 5 p.m.*

He's always been a charming little shit. I really thought I'd be angrier... seeing him... out in the wild, as it were. I thought I'd feel this real fury, this real... red. But I didn't, at all. There was a moment in time when he didn't exist and I was happy... well I was fine... and BAM. All of a sudden I'm back to whatever I was back when... Well back then.

You scan yourself and just feel embarrassed... that I'm not doing better? That I've not conquered Everest or started my own Etsy shop selling keyrings of cult comedies or some shit. Like, any ex, you run into any ex and you want to be able to tell them that you're doing better, eating healthier, feeling happier, shagging a celebrity, shagging a woman – I'm not a good liar.

I got good at it, for a bit, when I was with him...

guess it's really easy to lie when you've got no one to talk to. But then when you tell the truth to one person it just floods. Like you've been biting your tongue for so long and your mouth's filled with blood and then you open it to speak and... Floods. And you drown and erode in the pour-down that you're wishing on the person who made you lie in the first place.

Flood. Noun. A (usually disastrous) overflow of water from a lake or other body of water due to excessive rainfall or other input of water.

I mean, we're just water, right? So yeah, floods.

Except he's not water. He wasn't ever water. He's whiskey. Or bourbon, never knew the difference despite the endless explanations. But he's the burn in the back of your throat. He is the after taste. He is the hangover and I...

I was just after a good night out, when I met him. And I wasn't slutty back then, like, I resent that word because I could sleep with a billion people and you'd only call me a slut because you were jealous. Slut is a fictional thing made up to deny women sexual fulfilment. So not slutty but... I was, I think, a bit slutty, a bit unhappy and a little lost and just looking for a way to displace those feelings. I don't begrudge myself those years. I refuse to, because I do think you can do it – you can feed the five thousand – and still be happy, but equally you can just do it because you don't know what else to do. And I did have fun. And a lot of the shagging was really fucking fun, and good, and hot. Don't get me wrong, a lot of it was disastrous but I used to laugh. Big belly laughs during sex. It was fun. I was fun.

I was an explosion. A violent, hot, young explosion.

And I had the audacity to walk into his bar. His joint.

'Of all the gin joints in all the world...'

I was smashed, that night, but the memory is so cloudless.

I walked in, in a pleated gingham mini skirt, and a navy-blue high-neck T-shirt, but it was so dark it all looked black. I had my hair down, to my back then, and red lipstick. I think I was going for a bit of that classic-era, Taylor Swift vibe. I queued at the bar with my friends and –

You play over and over the what-ifs. What if we had decided that the line was too long and we'd just try the next place? What if one of us had forgotten ID? What if he wasn't on shift that night? What if I was out with Laura that night, who is infinitely sexier than I am? But a certain part of trauma, I think, is looking back at it and just seeing how inevitable it all is.

'Of all the gin joints in all the world, she had – HAD TO – walk into mine.'

– so eventually it's my turn in the queue and I ask for a Mojito and am only half paying attention to him because I'm chatting with Nina, but I hear him say,

'No.'

The fuck.

'I'm sorry what did you say?'

'No.'

And now I look at him and he's every bad-boy stereotype you can imagine. Older, tattooed, sexy as fuck. Left lip slightly turned up in a smile. I'm hooked. Utterly captured in the net. And his script is so slick because I couldn't even guess how many times he's said it,

'No. No no. Girls who look like you don't drink Mojitos.'

'Is that right?'

'Yeah, they're too common. Everyone orders a Mojito because they think it's classy, and they're too embarrassed to order what they really want which is a Screwdriver, or Sex on the Beach, or an Orgasm.'

I'm genuinely wet between the legs at this point. Gushing. Flooding. Caught.

'Girls who look like you don't get Mojitos.'

'And what exactly kind of girl do I look like?'

I look like a girl who's fucking loving it.

'You? You're…'

And he studies me, really studies me. His eyes are so clearly undressing me and he's not even trying to hide it. I let him, I actively encourage it. Shit me, he is so insanely hot.

'I think you're restless. You clearly have no idea exactly how stunning you are, what you do to people, what you do to men, what you're doing right now. I think you're mischievous and possibly the most serious person I'll ever meet. I think for the right person you'd open up like a flower.

Pause.

And I think you'd like a Negroni. And I think you'd like to give me your number.'

Now – honestly – tell me you'd say no to that. Tell me you'd turn down every hot barman in every shit romcom ever.

You wouldn't.

It's impossible.

You wouldn't.

I couldn't have.

PATRICIA *is still, in total silence. Her hands are shaking and she tries to steady them. She is trying not to cry.*

5 p.m.

PATRICIA *is choosing her outfits.*

> I need to look hot, goes without saying.
> Unobtainable hot. But I am discovering,
> upsettingly immediately, that there are two types
> of people in break-ups; those who get the Khloe
> Kardashian break-up body, and those who eat
> Galaxy Caramel until their souls feel a little less
> empty. It seems, unfortunately, I am the latter.
>
> URGH! Look at me. Look at me.
>
> I did this to myself.
>
> Fuck's sake.
>
> Fatty Patty.
>
> Fatty Patty.

PATRICIA *watches the clip, from* Nick and Nora's Infinate
Playlist, *of Nora ordering five martinis to cheer her up.*

> In hindsight, this spiel, all the 'type of girl I was',
> he was just telling me exactly what he wanted
> me to be. It was an instruction manual. The
> quintessential manic-pixie-dream girl. He's built
> her up in his mind, they all have, of course I'd
> never match up. You can never match up. You put
> reality next to a dream, it's never the same.
>
> I – uh – I gave him my number that night, and we
> slept together for two weeks then he made sure we
> were exclusive, then we slept together for a week
> more and he called me his girlfriend in front of his
> colleagues and that was that. Caged.

Not caged in that beautiful Jane Eyre, trapped-tiny-bird way, more circus animal. More upsetting. Caged.

There are things people don't tell you about abusive relationships. Like, it's not immediate. They don't hit you on the second date. You don't fall in love with a woman-beater, you fall in love with a fully-fledged human who one day lets you down in the most abominable way. One of the reasons I love... one of the reasons I thought he was alright was that he seemed really good at his job. Being a woman-beater doesn't mean you can't be good at your job. And they don't tell you that. And they don't tell you that there are, perhaps, more good days than bad days. It's just the bad days are quite a lot worse than other people's bad days so the scales... they don't even know how to tip. They're so confused.

Confuse. Verb. To thoroughly mix; to confound; to disorder.

The sex was always witchcraft. Actual sorcery, it was so good. Honest. It was... it felt like us two having sex was somehow sewed into the world turning. It was remarkable; some superhero... otherworldly sensation came over me when he wanted me. His hands. Feeling his hands press against my hips, or hold my wrists, or pull my hair. His hands made me shudder. The way he rocked inside of me; inexplicable. He fucked me so hard – like he needed it. He needed me and there is nothing sexier on this damn planet than that feeling. To be needed is to be wanted, and to be wanted is to have value... and that had been missing somewhere.

First time I was lying underneath him, first time he entered me whilst I was biting the fucking Nirvana tattoo on his forearm, he said 'you're in control.'

Curveball.

Like, at that point in my life, the only way I knew how to have sex was quickly and loudly so in a way, I do think it's my fault that we always had sex like that. I set the precedent... for the, lack of affection I guess.

Affection. Noun. A gentle feeling of fondness or liking.

If you want affection you should get a fucking dog Patricia.

Shouts.

Muum. Mum?

Beat.

Mummmm?

Beat.

What was the name of the dog we had when I was little?

Beat.

No. The dog.

Beat.

We did.

We did for a bit. It was Eleanor's, we had it for a few months.

Beat.

THE DOG.

Thanks Mum.

Oh yeah, so we did have a dog when I was really young but only whilst one of Mum's colleagues was off on her mad long honeymoon.

It was called Rowan?! A tiny little daschund called Rowan. It's not right. It's like a baby called Karen, or Keith, or Gary. It's not right.

Although a dog called Gary could be quite excellent. A sheepdog-style one would suit it I think. A collie? Are they called collies? I'd call one of them Gary.

It says it in that Greta Gerwig film, it says, and I'm fully aware I'm paraphrasing, but it's like, 'how completely ridiculous that we just accept the name our parents give to us.' But we do and then that's our name... forever. And it becomes so entwined with who you are the two things are inseparable to others.

If I ever have a daughter, I'd probably call her, at least her middle name, I'd call her Frances... because the kindest person I've ever known in my life is my mum, and you attach attributes to names and hope they seep into a person somehow.

I still can't watch *Emmerdale*, because to just hear his name spoken so calmly, so fondly, it's terrifying. It sends me into a complete panic.

Panic. Verb. To feel overwhelming fear.

Negronis, by the way, his drink, are fucking disgusting. Mojitos are refreshing, sweet and make you feel like summer. Negronis want you to stay inside and cry to a sad song. Negronis are lethal.

Beat.

Maybe I should just not go.

She listens to 'Happy Without Me' by Chloe x Halle.

PATRICIA *gets changed into a very 'dressy' outfit.*

PATRICIA *gets changed into jeans and a T-shirt.*

PATRICIA *gets changed into a gingham skirt and high-neck navy-blue T-shirt. She looks at herself. Her breathing begins to escalate. She calms herself down and changes into her pyjamas.*

> I'm scared if I talk to you about the hitting, the… all of it… you'll judge me.

Pause.

> Okay, so when I was ten I had the biggest, most massively blatant crush on Ashley Riley; everyone called him Ash. This crush was humungous. It was so big. It was love. It all started because he said he liked the band Korn, and I pretended I did too because I'd seen it on one of my brother's hoodies.

> Now – I don't know if you've ever listened to the band Korn, but their music is… how can I put this cordially… it is so vile that it makes whatever song they use in them prison torture techniques seem like a really lovely ditty. But Korn was our bond, and I was obsessed by Ash. I used to scribble 'Patricia Riley' in my schoolbooks over and over again, and I did it like really big so the person next to me would see and it would Chinese-whisper its way back to Ash.

> So about a week before prom – which is a stupid Americanism we've stupidly adopted because we're stupid, and this was especially dumb as it was prom for the kids going from primary to secondary school – stupid. Anyways it was a week before prom – ew – and Ash walked over to me,

cock first, or like at ten years old… nub first, in
the playground and asked me to go with him. I
screamed yes in his face and then ran to tell all my
girlfriends who were at the tuck shop.

Euphoria.

It felt so spectacular; I was just ear to ear smiling.
This rad dreamboat who also liked weird heavy-
metal music, that I obviously adored too, was
into me! He was into me! My self-confidence
reached a new high. It was… I was so happy. That
night I went to Claire's Accessories and got all
the fluorescent butterfly hair clips that five pound
pocket money could buy. I was going to strut into
that prom, on the arm of Ashley Riley, looking like
the ten-year-old dog's bollocks.

And I did.

Except half an hour later I spotted him, in the
middle of the fucking sports hall, snogging
Edith Williams. Edith Williams has always been
a prize-A little prick. She constantly had mud
under her fingernails, which she would scrape out
with her teeth and then swallow. Once, when we
were six, she farted in the Christmas assembly.
Right in the middle of 'Little Donkey'. Bloody
disrespectful. Why on earth mega-god Ash wanted
to snog her I will never know. And it wasn't a
snog, it was more of a grooming of each other's
face with saliva and tongues – like how they kiss in
The Lion King, which I imagine is the only mildly
romantic film either of them had ever seen at that
point.

My initial, immediate reaction is why was no one
stepping in to stop this abomination. Where were
the sodding teachers? But my second reaction;

heartbreak. I was so gutted. Inconsolable. I made
the dinner lady call my mum to come pick me up.

I was so broken. I listened to 'Deeper Shade of
Blue' for days and days – great track by the way.
Severely underrated. But then it was summer
holidays… it was the summer of that song 'Bad
Day' by Daniel Powter. Fucking LOL. And my
spirits went up. Summer with friends and inflatable
pools in back gardens and super soakers and going
to the cinema to watch *Pirates of the Caribbean*. It
was perfect.

Come September I couldn't even remember Ashley
Blah Blah Blah's second name.

Pause.

I still really struggle to talk about it, the hitting,
and time does heal a lot but not everything, so it's
still really hard.

It's like my abortion. I'm not at all embarrassed
about my abortion, nor do I feel guilty about it, but
I don't talk about it because you just don't know
how people might react. They might judge you
they might not, they might gasp, they might have
had one too – one in four, bitches – but there is no
real way of knowing beforehand. None.

It's like…

Shame. Noun. A painful feeling of humiliation or
distress caused by the consciousness of wrong or
foolish behaviour.

So, by definition, if I feel shame then it was wrong
behaviour? But no. I don't think it was.

So, you pick and choose when you talk about the
hitting. Because you can. Because you, and only

you, can make that choice and that's power. But
you can never not feel it. You can never not feel...

You know what I don't actually feel the hit
consistently. The stinging in the cheek, the throb
in your stomach, that's not what I feel. What I feel,
all day every day is the short, sudden tension in my
neck when I strained it, when I knew he was going
to hit me. The moment of anticipation as he raises
his big, tattooed arm, and you know what's coming
so your entire body seizes up. That's what I feel.

All the time.

It's the same place for the other stuff too – like
he pushes you; neck tenses. He grabs you; neck
tenses. He scratches you; neck tenses. It's quite
smart really... it's like in that moment your neck
understands that your body has to disconnect from
your brain. You have to be able to NOT THINK.
Not feel. In that moment, logicise it after. It's
smart.

Mum wanted me to go see a therapist but it's
not for me. Some greying white guy in a patchy
jumper asking to speak about my parents. I think
me being with an abusive man probably has a hell
of a lot more to do with his parents that with mine.

You'd like her better than me, Mum. She's softer.
Really caring and soft.

3 p.m.

Mum, I'm not going to want dinner tonight. I'm going out.

Just with some friends for dinner.

Laura.

She was, she just got back.

Yes she did. Why would I lie?

I'm not lying, I'm going out for dinner with Laura.

Oh.

This is... ugh... this is why I hate small towns. It's none of her damn business is it.

Is it?!

Actually it's none of yours! I just wanted to be polite and tell you not to waste food on me tonight. Now, I'm going to get ready.

No, no, no don't try and guilt trip me, that's bullshit.

I'll swear whenever the fuck I want to swear.

Is it or is it not my choice?

Is it or is it not my choice?

YOU CONTROLLING BITCH IS IT OR IS IT NOT MY CHOICE?

Right.

If I have something to say to him, I get to say it on my terms. You don't get a say in this. No one gets a fucking say in this, except me.

I'm going to go get ready.

Don't cook for me.

7 p.m.

Okay.

The first time hurt the second most. The second time hurt the first most, because the second time is when you realise it's not a one-time thing. But the first time was weird. We were about four months in and I brought my friend Paddy out for drinks at his bar because it was the only one I was allowed to drink at.

He never said that outright but any time I went anywhere else it was all, 'why would you do that, you can drink for free with me?' I got the hint.

Now Paddy is as gay as George Clooney – I back myself on that – but he was male, and that was his first mistake. Other mistakes Paddy made during that evening were speaking to me, speaking to him, existing…

He and I weren't living together at that point, but at 4 a.m. my doorbell starts going off simultaneously with my phone.

Dread. Verb. Anticipate with great apprehension and fear.

As soon as I open the door to him –

'What the fuck are you playing at? My colleagues were laughing at me all night. They all watched you dancing with him. They all watched you acting like… slutty… making a fucking fool of yourself. Making a fool of me. Why would you bring someone to my bar to do that to me? What kind of person are you.'

You can talk all the sense you want; he's always going to whack you one. Always. No matter. And he did.

Think it was after my fifth or sixth protest, telling him how stupid he was being, literally telling him Patrick's gay.

He hits me.

I think he anticipated more of a flinch from me or something, or maybe because he was drunk his aim was off, but his fist lands right on my ear.

It hurt so much.

It hurt so much.

She listens to 'Midnight Train to Georgia' by Gladys Knight and the Pips.

PATRICIA *necks the Mojito in one.*

PATRICIA *continues to apply her make up.*

See, he asked me to dinner, which means he must have something to say. Right? He could have so easily just let me walk past, or just asked how I was, but asking someone for dinner, that's intentional. That's a statement. It's brave. That's brave. So he must have something he needs to tell me?

I would. I'd be really happy for him if he sought out help. Because we were, we were good sometimes. Most of the time. A lot of the time.

Ugh. No sorry. Enough of that.

But it was nice to see him, a little bit of me was happy to see him. Happy to see him smiling. You can't just turn off caring about someone, and he's probably feeling that too, that's probably why he wants to sit down for dinner together. You don't just stop loving someone.

God. I can hear myself. Sorry, I can hear myself. You must all think I'm a right pathetic little dweeb. Sorry! Sorry! I'll be cheerier.

Sorry.

It just, occasionally it is so tempting. Part of you wants to lean into it; give the people the pain they want. Exist only in the saddest of states. That ache in your bones, sting-in-your-tear-duct kind of sad. It is the saddest thing to beg someone to love you the way you love them. It is a suffering that gets in your system and spreads like a cancer. To lean into that, to be the 'sad' the world needs you to be so they can understand, it's so tempting.

But it's a state. It's not a person. Who I am is better than this.

I was very determined to be better than this. I am very determined to be better than this.

Better. Adjective. More desirable, satisfactory or effective.

When you come out of something like that, a relationship like that, everyone just asks you so many questions about stuff that... it's so difficult. Actually, not difficult, it's just really fucking rude. Why? Why didn't you leave? Why didn't you tell someone? Why didn't you hit him back? How long

was this going on? How often was this going on?
What provoked it? What did he say afterwards?
Why? How? What? Why? How? What? Why?

It's overwhelming. It is incredibly overwhelming,
and the most frustrating thing is you can't answer
– what's the point. People don't want the answer
they just want to ask the question. There is no
real way of explaining an abusive relationship to
someone who hasn't been in one. I promise you
now it is impossible, because that person will
never be able to fathom the conflict that goes on
inside your own head.

I tried for a bit, I got so frustrated that I couldn't…
articulate myself well enough to extract real
empathy from people. So I learnt all these useless
word definitions thinking it was the way I was
talking. I was describing it wrong. I was saying
abusive wrong. I was saying hit wrong. But course
I fucking wasn't, but it just means something very
different to me than it does to you.

Something very fucking different.

Different. Adjective. Not the same as another or
each other; unlike in nature, form, or quality.

Right, so I could describe the second time he hit
me, the worse time, I could describe that to you.
But would it make any difference? Why do you
need to know? We were in the kitchen. It was
afternoon. He shoved me against a fridge and then
hit me, for… and I mean this literally… no reason
at all. The next day, I apologised to him. My head
sees logic in that. Your head doesn't. I get that you
don't get it. I'm happy that you don't get it because
that means that you haven't been through it, so…
yay.

Abuse. Noun. Cruel and violent treatment of a
person or animal.

Cruel. Adjective. Wilfully causing pain or suffering
to others, or feeling no concern about it.

What word is the right word? When does it sink
in for people what I went through? And why do
people need to know – to feel better that it's not
them? Like...

There's these bullshit Pinterest motivational
quotes, that people cling to as solutions; crap like,
'there is a blessing in the storm.' WHY CAN'T
PEOPLE JUST GET IT?

Sometimes you don't need explanations. It is what
it is. There's no deeper meaning here. There's no
silver lining. It is what it is. It was what it was.

You don't understand.

You can't understand.

All you've got is me and my words and they're not
enough.

Hurt. Anger. Pain. Excitement. Love. Tenderness.
Vulnerable. Need. Want. Pain. Punch. Kick. Sex.
Love. Hard. Lonely. Alone. Totally alone. Trust.
Safe. Security. Passion. Hurt. Violence. Anger.
Silence. Endings. Sleep. Isolation. Manipulation.
Clever. Fun. Inexplicable.

Inexplicable.

PATRICIA *changes out of her pyjamas into a skirt and black
roll neck top.*

8 p.m.

Fuck I've got to get going.

Oh my days, oh my actual days I feel so sick.

Shit. Shit. Shit. Shit. Shit. Shit. Shit. Shit. Shit.

It's weird this very much feels like a first date, but equally feels like Jesus's Last Supper.

What if I walk in there, look at him, and just immediately throw up. Actually, no, that would be quite good wouldn't it.

Okay. I've got to move haven't I. Okay. Okay. Okay.

Oh my god this is so scary. I cannot explain my heart right now.

I know… I know you think I shouldn't go. I do know that, but these aren't your choices. This isn't your life, this isn't your predicament. How could you possibly know what you'd do?

The fact is loving him was simply the most exquisite form of self-destruction. Doesn't mean it wasn't love. It's all the opposite of simple and…

Breathing. Deep breathing. Okay okay okay.

One year ago.

Mum? Mum? MUM? Are you in?

It's Patricia.

Mum?

Oh hey.

Yeah. I'm fine. I'm fine.

Mum I promise I'm fine, I just I need to um…
could I…

No Mum please –

You know what Mum, could I just have a cup of
tea?

Thank you.

Long pause.

(*Shouting offstage.*) Mum can you hear me through
there?

No, no. Don't come back in. But can you hear me
through there, yeah?

Would you stay there?

It's easier, for me to talk. So would you stay there?

Okay thank you.

I think… I think I need to stay here at home for
a while… maybe for a long while. I think I need
some care; proper caring care that I think you can
only get from mums. And I'm going to tell you,
but I need you to promise me – promise me – that
you're not going to ask why I didn't leave sooner.
Okay?

Promise?

Okay.

Sorry.

Pause.

He – fuck – he hit me. A lot. He has hit me a lot,
for a really long time. At first I think I was just
really, really dumb but at the end I was just really,
really scared.

No! No. Do not come in. I'm still talking.

I genuinely believed... each time I genuinely
believed it wasn't going to happen again. Then
I realised that it inevitably was going to happen
again, but I knew exactly how long it would last,
and then it would end. And I know – I know that
sounds like madness but it's not like... that's not
like all it was all the time.

I loved him. I love him so much. The fact is I love
him more than I love myself and that's so, so sad. I
know how sad that is but that's the only way I can
put this in a comprehendible way. I love him more
than I love me, so I made it okay. Mum, I made it
okay for so long and I'm so mad at myself for it.

I'm here now. I'm here now, that matters so please
don't look at me any differently because...

I feel like such a shit person Mum. Like I failed so
bad.

So can I have a hug? Can you come in now? Can I
have a hug?

PATRICIA*'s body tenses and her eyes close as she is hugged
by her mother.*

Don't cry. Don't be daft don't cry. If I'm not crying
then you shouldn't be crying.

Can I live here for a bit?

He'll come to the house, he'll be here, and he'll
come to the house. Don't let me go with him.
Please. Please Mum, because I'll want to, do not
let me leave with him, barricade me in a room if
you have to.

> I want to be here and home with you.
>
> Just me and you.
>
> Promise?

8.15 p.m.

PATRICIA *stands, lonely, staring out into space. She focuses on steadying her breath.*

PATRICIA *lights a cigarette and talks steadily.*

> I know what I'm going to say. Course I do. I've known what I've wanted to say since the first time he hit me, since the first time I left. And yeah it might not affect him in the slightest. It might not, but it might, because men like that someone has to tell them at some point, and the fact is it shouldn't be me that has to say it to him but it is, here I am, outside this fucking restaurant and it's going to be said.
>
> I'm going to march in there, I'm going to march in and not even sit down. No no. I will sit down. I will act all calm, I will order a very large glass of red wine, but if he asks me questions I'll say nothing. I'll let his temper, his agitation, build. I'll look bored, and then once my red wine comes, I'll glance up, nonchalant, but purposeful. I'll look him straight in the fucking eye and I'll say... I'll say,
>
> 'When the person you love hits you it hurts. When the person you love alters your entire being, it is a fatality to the soul. You made me needy, you made

me cold; you made me believe I was unlovable.
But I am none of those things. You are. I was just
a fuckable thing you could project onto. I was just
a cunt you used as a distraction for your deep,
deep misery, which I hope you never cure. I want
no good things for you. I have value and worth
and none of it is dependent on you. None of it is
dependent on anyone, it is just mine. I am entirely
my own; I am messy and brilliant and that is
enough. I may not be phenomenal and the fact is I
may not change the world, but I'm not letting you
change me any more.'

Pause.

I am going to say that to him. I think I can. I can be
strong enough, I think I can be strong enough.

No chickening out this time. I can. I think I can. I
really believe I might be able to.

I think I can.

Imagine if I'd said that in the first place. Just had
the strength to look the guy dead in the eye and tell
him the truth. The truth he's so terrified of hearing
but the truth someone really needs to tell him.

1 p.m.

Shit.

Hi.

Oh my God.

Hi, no I've said that.

Hi.

Pause.

I... I um... I didn't know you were back. I just –

no you go –

You're a cunt.

You are. You're a total asshole. I hate you so much.
I hate you so Goddamn much. I am really happy
to see you, that's surprised me, it's surprising
how happy to see you I am – but simultaneously
it's weird to see you because this whole time I've
blissfully been imagining you dead, alone in a flat
that smells of dick and weed and having your flesh
picked off your bones by cats. Cats that aren't even
yours. The neighbour's cats.

Did you know? Like, the from the first time we
met, or the first time we kissed, or the first time
we had sex... did you know then how much you
were going to hurt me? Was there always an expiry
date on your niceness or was it random? Really.
I'd like to know. And in the future maybe tell the
girl that you're going to punch her before you take
her out on a date, because then, you know, she can
make an educated decision whether or not she's
got enough energy and willpower to waste two
years in misery and then an endless stretch of time
afterwards attempting to recover from you.

Endless.

I could. I could tell you how insecure you are and
how much you want to sleep with your mother. But
I won't. What's the point?

You are soulless. You are heroin. And you are
fever. And you are gunfire. And you are cupboards
closing too loud and too quickly. And you are debt.
Nothing good.

Look, I'm really tired. And really sad. And
I'm going to head home because Mum's made
vegetarian lasagne so...

I think if I had the balls to really mean it I'd tell
you that when the person you love hits you it hurts.
When the person you love alters your entire being,
it is a fatality to the soul. You made me needy,
you made me cold; you made me believe I was
unlovable. But I am none of those things. You are.
I was just a fuckable thing you could project onto.
I was just a cunt you used as a distraction for your
deep, deep misery, which I hope you never cure.
I want no good things for you. I have value and
worth and none of it is dependent on you. None
of it is dependent on anyone, it is just mine. I am
entirely my own, and that is enough.

I really love you still. It's so confusing. I think
about you all the time. I still wished you kissed my
neck and held my hand too tight, but I never want
you to do those things again. It's so confusing.

When I left you, I could not say your name out
loud. I don't think I've said your name out loud for
the past year. That is the only way I can articulate
the mess you left me in. I could not say a name
out loud. You ripped away my voice. I don't fall
into a crumbling wreck on the floor each day, I
don't experience haunting flashbacks in the aisles
of Tesco and drop soup cans in slow motion. I am
a person. I am a person who removed your name
from my mouth... and it's been carnage.

I just want it all erased. I think. Right.

Like I said... lasagne.

And garlic bread actually so...

Bye.

A moment in time.

The battered woman must not be strong. She
must not be healthy, and she most certainly must
not look like you. The battered woman must
not be funny, unless using humour as a defence
mechanism. She must not hold down a respectable
job or be in a position power. The battered woman
is meek, feeble and apologetic. The battered
woman is not your boss. She is most likely a
waitress or sales assistant; something you are not.
The battered woman is white. The battered woman
is blonde, and thin. She is a bit too thin. That
battered woman is worryingly thin. The battered
woman must leave after the first time she is hit, or
never leave at all. The battered woman does not
have a close group of female friends. The battered
woman does not brunch.

The battered woman must not be real. The battered
woman must not be your friend, nor your relative.
She might be a girl you went to school with a long
time ago and have constantly meant to reach out
to, but you've never got around to it. The battered
woman is not a daughter. The battered woman is
not a sister.

The battered woman is not you.

The battered woman is not me.

The battered woman is not –

8.30 p.m.

Shit.

Hi.

Blackout.